Theatre for Development Project

Theatre for Development Project

Delma Jackson

To order additional copies of this book, contact:
Xlibris
844-714-8691
www.Xlibris.com
Orders@Xlibris.com
845488

CONTENTS

To the people of Mnlonganzila Village

Chapter 1

Cultural Components of Social Work Education

Introduction

As a social worker in America, I have been exposed to various creative techniques that have been used successfully when working with clients. Skillfully trained social workers use their expertise to assist in creating positive and constructive change in the lives of the underprivileged and others in need; thus such social work models as casework, community organization, group work, and administration are the foundation of social work training.

The social worker makes use of his or her skill, knowledge, and training to extract the client's participation in and understand of his/ her or community need for change. This change occurs through self-help, social service, or agency support available with the social worker as facilitator.

This facilitator function of the social work profession has expanded as the nature of the problems being addressed has changed. Individual, community, and world problems have become more complex; for example, governments are less able to control border crossing for other populations outside their respective countries. Migration may contribute to the spread of disease or poverty. Natural disasters, war, and poverty are now more common and more likely to create a need for refugee assistance. These dynamics are cultural complexities, which contribute to the need for more in-depth understanding as well as a new concept of the culture of poverty. Such mobility and change within the world has globalized poverty and created what seems to be more resistant strands of poverty, and the need for additional skills for addressing these concerns.

Social work in this new and more global society must be culturally sensitive, bilingual, and have a diverse cultural skillset. They need greater understanding of how globalization and economic forces impact the lives of all people, specifically the world's poor. Poverty in today's world includes issues of food security, pure water, natural disasters, literacy, and disease. World problems of this sort now impact the economic viability of surrounding countries, brain drain from the residents of the Global South, and other development issues.

America, as well as other Western nations, is the sole focus of illegal migration from poorer nations for education, work, and survival opportunities. This is not to say that previously taught social work techniques are no longer applicable. These world changes offer the social worker opportunities to make significant contributions worldwide as well as opportunities to learn from helping skills of other cultures. Western social work is expanding to include a broader understanding of homelessness, migration, and world economics and how they impact the profession in its work with families, individuals, and communities worldwide.

Internationally, the concept of development is often referred to when discussing underdeveloped or undeveloped countries of the residents of the Global South and now Eastern Europe, and Central America However, I submit that the dynamics of development apply in our own backyards. The characteristics of development can and should be applied to any experience, which significantly limit human potential. Lack of development regionally, in education or a housing project, can be just as limiting in human potential. All of these development issues deserve social work attention, skill, and commitment.

Skill and commitment demand continuous infusion of techniques that enable the profession to fulfill its mission. Although not a new find, I feel Theatre for Development (TFD) is compatible as a resource for social work intervention. TFD offers the social worker another way of starting where the client is and facilitating the clients participation in the change process.

I participated in just such a program with the Theatre Arts Department of the University of Dar es Salaam. The training process for this work began in the classroom. We were trained in Kiswahili language skills, TFD history, and process before proceeding to the villages in which I worked. I will share what I learned about the use of TFD, as well as research examining the lives of rural Tanzanian women.

Theatre For Development Research Process

- **Familiarization**: This stage involves facilitators getting to know the villagers and vice versa. Sharing about the purpose of the project occurs after a written request and authorization has been made and received to and from village administrators.
- **Data Collection**: Stage two involves a door-to-door collection of information about concerns of villagers.
- **Data Analysis**: Facilitators discussing and analyzing community issues, setting priorities about which are the most important to the villagers and the real heart of the problems. As a scientific tool to help with this process, charts were used in order to maintain focus and objectivity.
- **Theatre Creation**
- **Performance**
- **Post-performance discussion**

The Village of Mlonganzila Project

Mlonganzila is a village in Tanzania East Africa. It is located thirty miles southwest of the city of Dar es Salaam (after the village of Embezi and Kibombaba but before Kiluvya). Residing in the village are 250 homes and approximately one thousand people. The population of this village earns approximately one hundred US dollars per year (exchange rate: TSh 800 to $1). The average time of residence for village members is approximately fifteen to twenty-five years. Over 90 percent of villagers live without electricity, running water, clean well water supply, inside plumbing, schools, health facilities, permanent homes, or crops and stable incomes.

The request for assistance in the village came to professor Nyoni of the theatre department. A university agriculture employee and village made the request for the residents. After securing proper written permission from village administrators, the following schedule was developed for the project:

- Familiarization: Days: 3–5
- Data Collection: Days: 5–7
- Data Analysis: Days: 9–11
- Theatre Creation: Days: 12–22
- Performance: Days: 1
- Post-performance discussion and follow-up: Days 1

Familiarization

The familiarization process really began with the university's theatre group's introduction to "seven struggles", the name of the village theatre group established several months ago. Each meeting with this group began with warm-up activities of songs, games, and dances. As we became more comfortable with each other, considerable sharing took place. We learned more about their previous theatre activities as a newly developed group. They shared their perception of what the problems were in the village. The problems identified during this stage of the project were as follows:

- Lack of health facilities
- No clean water source
- No employment
- Long distances for most of the smaller school children to travel
- Young girls were forced into prostitution because of family poverty
- Teenage pregnancy
- No communication system for the villagers.

During our discussions with Seven Struggle, it was decided that we would team up together for the familiarization part of the project and that they would present a performance at the end. The teaming up process was decided because of their knowledge of the community etc. We continued in teams, going from door to door. We explained who we were and what we were, as students from the university and the United States, doing in the village. These were short, well received visits. Most of the villagers were glad to have visitors and none had ever seen a black person from the United States before.

This early phase of this process was used to cement relationships and to build goodwill within the community, hopefully eliciting community spirit, cooperation, and trust.

An elderly lady asked Dr. Nyoni, our director, for assistance with rebuilding parts of her home. The house was made of clay and wooden polls cut from trees, and she shared this home with an older sister. This house was located on a lot immediately behind a one-room brick home belonging to her brother. The instructor from Howard University, Dr. Nyoni, and myself contributed TSC10,000 for materials, after viewing the work that needed to be done. The money was given to the brother and he secured the materials.

Our class and Seven Struggle spent two days rebuilding walls for the house. The brother disappeared during the work process and never provided oversight or assistance. This was very surprising and unusual behavior. Later in the process, it was decided that this had been a bad decision. The objective was to build goodwill; however, it was also to galvanize the community support. No other community members helped. Nor did the occupants of the house of the brother show the proper gratitude according to cultural expectations. In fact, the brother and sister continued to request other assistance, such as additional building projects and food money.

Additionally, others in the community then began to identify their individual needs as opposed to working in a collective way to address them. The property owners, according to Dr. Nyoni, should be considered mentally ill because she was acting outside the proper cultural context by not sharing fruit from her orange tree, showing anger and ingratitude for our efforts. He also pointed out that they had no children, and this in itself may have been a sign of some genetic problem.

Another goodwill gesture of the community came as we were finishing the building. We were notified of a death of one of the Muslim residents, a woman. As a result, we were unable to meet with community members as had been scheduled. We were then instructed to go to the home of the family and give condolences and money. We visited on the day of the funeral sitting on the floor with the women for several hours because we as women could not attend the burial service, which is attended only by the men.

Data Collection

During this phase, we continued to team up with Seven struggle. First, we reviewed the plan for the day after warm-up exercises. Each team was accompanied by one of three university students who had been hired to work with this project. Mr. Godfrey Mngeraza accompanied me because he was a graduate and fluent in English.

My social work interviewing knowledge led me to develop a questionnaire that I thought would give me the necessary data. However, the questions addressed individual household demographics as opposed to question about collective problems of the village. Some of the questions asked were the name, age, education of household members, and identification of health status by asking question on aches, pains, and worries. Other questions asked covered issues of abuse, managing difficult chores alone, length of marriage, second wives, lovers, and confidantes.

I tried to ascertain some sense of the individual mental health status by asking about unusual crying, headaches, if husbands loved their wives, etc. I found these questions did provide some basic information but did not give me a clue into the real day-to-day living situation of the villagers. I learned much more through observation, building relationships, and experiencing than asking.

Through observation, I noted that most of the children had runny noses, skin rashes, and yellow eyes, and played in the dust and dirt at all times and drank water stored in large oil drums. Most families ate once a day because of limited food supplies.

I listened as an old woman talked about not having help to get water from the well, money for doctors, or money to return to her home village where she could live with their family and be cared for. Villagers talked about land and boundary disputes with the army and no compensation. They were forbidden to build permanent homes or plant permanent crops. Their small children spent the day travelling to a faraway school (I watched them returning home at dark) or didn't go at all.

Our data collection showed that school, land disputes, medical facility, and water were the greatest concerns. During meetings with the village women, I asked what they did to earn money and how they spent their days. I also asked how they planned to deal with the threat of famine.

The groups of village women admitted to doing little but, at one point, showed me some weaving. Several were able to make into mats, which could be sold. However, they had only sold one. In discussions about helping and teaching each other, they said they have never worked like that and that most things in the village operated on a cash only basis; however, these women had no money. At this point, I began to feel that there were other circumstances, which had some impact on this group, that I just did not understand.

I began to find some of the answers to my questions in the literature written about Tanzanian government initiatives of 1973. In an article by Ede, Semboja, et al., initiatives that include naturalization of economic sectors and relocation of the rural population through a villagization process occurred. According to the study,

> the suppression of private business both redirected the opportunities for peasants to diversify as producers and increased the prices they faced as consumers. The combination of price controls, import controls, and investment in industry led to increasingly severe shortages in non-agricultural consumer goods in rural areas. Also, notable was the fact that increased in crop prices on world markets were not passed on to farmers. (p.65)

There were many such policy measures, which had implication for poverty. As recorded, "for one thing, the participation of peasants and the urban self-employed in income - generating activities was inhibited, with a consequent narrowing of the range of income sources having a negative impact on rural and urban agents scope for getting out of poverty" (p.65).

Thus, the major factors behind persistent poverty in Tanzania are failed policies to promote economic growth, give support to the agricultural sector, rural industries, and disrupted local institutions. Thus, poverty in the urban and rural sectors has increased (ibid.).

Additionally, a primary concern of the villagers was the lack of any health facility. Christopher J. Comoro of the University of Dar es Salaam addressed this concern. According to Comoro, "one of the central stumbling blocks facing modern medicine is that doctors approach the human body with the same way Western science has always approached nature. They see it as a mechanism, like a clock, in which each part may be examined independently of each others. This view enables medicine to achieve a fuller understand of each disease but neglects the body as a whole and ignores the effect of illness on the patients emotional state" (p.22).

This explanation helped to explain, for me, the gap between the answer to my questions and the nebulous sense of emotional well-being in the village women. When discussing the alternative treatment health possibilities with Seven Struggle, they said most people do not trust traditional healers. However, after some discussion, it was acknowledged that there are categories of traditional healers and that villagers use them.

In her article on traditional medicine, Deborah Meachan shares insights by priestesses about the role of traditional healers and their impact in the developing world. In relation to mental health, she states, "black magic or witchcraft, can cause a range of maladies including evil eye, harassment by spirits, a string of bad luck, mental illness and physical ailments, all of which can significantly impact an individuals well being and long term health" (p.34).

Our research during this process did reveal several contacts by villagers with traditional healers in order to solve or clarify a perceived problem. Although in his paper on traditional medical and Western medicine practice in Tanzania, Professor Comoro adds insight on the impact of colonialism, Christianity, and Western medicine on health care in Tanzania. According to Professor Comoro, when addressing services where rural, transportation, cultural, and a variety of health needs, "the present epoch is experiencing more state tolerance towards traditional health seeking behavior. As individuals, many including those occupying important positions in the state hierarchy occasionally rely on traditional health seeking behavior methods, which were formally rejected by the state powers, that they had superseded" (p.164).

Both approaches, traditional and Western medicine, seem to acknowledge a receptivity to the need for a more flexible working relationship. Priestesses Mirian and Oswan Chamani state, "traditional healers can not, and do not attempt, to replace biomedicine, but they can play an important role in the larger health care structure" (p.36). Additionally, Comoro quotes a young doctor as saying, "we doctors are just not ready to handle the patient and his family in extreme situations. Such specialization in the Tanzanian setting may not have all the answers to the health-seeking behavior of the people" (p.22).

He continues by asserting that economic achievement through resettling peasantry (which may have been the case of Mlonganzila about 1976 and will certainly be the case if the army pursues the takeover of village lands) has not provided social services with substantial self-sustaining ability into this new century.

Thus, in many ways, the data collection process of popular theatre development is right on target. It is recommended in the Development Policy Review that "much needs to be done in terms of research and analysis to unravel the puzzle's surrounding the poverty situation in the country. This is predicated on having in place high quality data, namely data based on actual observation of individual drawn from household surveys" (p. 67).

Thus far, data collection techniques revealed ongoing problems for this rural village population, which include the question of village leadership's ability to address their collective needs.

Data Analysis

The data analysis process involved meeting with Seven Struggle, classroom discussions, and discussions with village leaders. It was decided that villagers were primarily concerned with

- health facilities (the way they are treated as poor, often dirty farmers by hospital personnel in other communities);
- not having access to clean water (stress contributes to arguing between women at the well); and
- lack of a local school for the youngest children and land disputes with the army (the women say army harassment includes sexual contact with the women. They have not told their husbands).

Discussion of data did not include information on government economic policies related to rural living, history of Tanzanian development overall, or the impact of social forces, such as divorce on village life. Additionally, cultural and village administrative information that might influence the data collection and analysis process was not stressed. Some of these concerns were

- men and women would not meet together;
- in the home, men had to give permission for women to be questioned;
- Muslim men could have as many as four wives; and
- village administration was hierarchical and heavily influenced by power positions of former army officials in leadership positions.

Theatre Creation

This component of our project, while lively, proved to be the most difficult. Seven Struggle, although a theatre group, had great difficulty developing a presentation form that would demonstrate community problems. They were grateful for our assistance, but I think something was lost in the translation or quite possibly, and most likely, they were not use to direction. They were described as being without technical skill, discipline, and structure. This made our two directors jobs much more difficult.

By putting together an artistic presentation, the community is stimulated to look, analyze, and formulate some approach to addressing community problems. During the creative process, we all participated as Seven Struggle worked with our Howard University theatre professor.

The women's group, on the other hand, did a bit better. All group meeting began with singing and dance presentations prior to discussion. This stimulated friendship and a mood for sharing. We sang some American songs for them and joined in as they danced, trying to learn the steps. They were pleased as they laughed at our efforts.

They began to communicate stories about their lives, some of which had not been shared with the men. These stories revealed the stress of collecting water before dawn, sexual overtures from soldiers, and their lack of skill and knowledge about how to work in a supportive and collective fashion, even in the face of famine.

As for the men's group, a clear presentation of their contributions nor their proposed presentation was ever elaborated upon. However, it was discussed when the administrator warned them not to participate because our questions proved to be upsetting to the establishment.

There were some anxious times, as we realized that our intervention might be forces out. Our being there and involving the villagers in open dialogue about their living situation, threatened some village leaders. One headman went to the men of the community, warning them that he would still be there after (we Americans) had gone back home; he advised them not to participate. It took several meetings between Dr. Nyoni and other leaders to save the day. The presentation was then scaled down to be preformed for just one hamlet of Mlonganzila and not the total village.

Chapter 2

A Professional Growth: Social Workers as Managers in Bridging the Gap for Professional Development in Tanzania

Introduction

Social work profession in Tanzania is weak and mostly confused with other disciplines, such as sociology and community development. Traditional social work in Tanzania mainly focuses on providing services to people in need, mostly at individual and family levels, group and community levels, and more recently, at the level of organizations. The social worker is called upon when something in the basic social functioning area threatens the life and development of a person as a social human being.

I. The Social Work Development in Tanzania

Efforts Provided by the Government of Tanzania by Department of Social Welfare (DSW) under the Ministry of Health and Social Welfare
The Department of Social Welfare (DSW) of the Ministry of Health and Social Welfare (MOHSW) is tasked with protecting orphans and vunerable children (OVC) and ensuring their access to basic services.

It is responsible for policy guidance in the area of social welfare with a focus on ensuring adequate and quality care and timely social welfare services to vulnerable groups. Its key targets are the elderly, people with disabilities, and vulnerable children.

The DSW, however, faces a number of challenges in fulfilling its functions. The DSW has inadequate technical, management, organizational, financial, and human capacity. Although there is an act that established the department, the instrument does not provide enough details about its (the department's) roles. Improvement is needed in data collection, management and utilization, training and staff development, documentation, research and analysis, resource mobilization, and advocacy strategy, as there is an overdependence on external funding to deliver its mandate. Understaffing seriously impinges on delivery of mandate at national and decentralized level—many districts do not even have one social welfare officer. There is a low profile of the department within the ministry and inadequate understanding of its functions and roles. Low visibility impacts resources allocation from government, among other things (Ernst and Young 2009). Many social welfare resources and functions were recently decentralized from the national to district levels in an effort to address the needs of OVC and other vulnerable groups more effectively.

Currently, there is no formal strategy for strengthening the social welfare workforce in Tanzania. However, DSW led the development of a first phase of National Costed Plan of Action (NCPA), which is a guide to outline the identification of most vulnerable children, coordinate the efforts of nongovernmental organizations (NGOs), mobilize resources, and implement a national data management system (DMS). The second phase of the NCPA is underway, and it includes plans for developing a social welfare workforce strategy in Tanzania. This will be a response toward strengthening social welfare workforce since half of districts in Tanzania have district social welfare officers. To fill in this gap, the government has been largely relying on paraprofessional social workers, including community volunteers, community justice facilitators, and the para social workers (PSWs).

II. Development of PSW Training Program in Tanzania

The Social Work–HIV/AIDS Partnership Project for Orphans and Vulnerable Children in Tanzania was first piloted in 2006 (see www. TwinningagainstAIDS.org). The model that trains community-based caregivers in key social work and child development skills is currently being replicated in Ethiopia and Nigeria. The program was established as a result of the assessment, which was done by the Department of Social Welfare, that the para social work training was to be a strategy to decentralize the social welfare services in order to ensure quality OVC services to the communities and families. But also Tanzania's welfare system was severely overstretched by the AIDS epidemic, and it lacks sufficient social workers to address needs. Lastly, it was noticed that there was a shortage of trained human resources in the health and social services sectors.

Due to these reasons, para social workers were trained at the village and ward level so as to help the social welfare officers who work at district level. The para social workers assess the needs, provide care and support, do referrals of clients to various services, and also provide ongoing follow-up care in the delivery of foundational social welfare services in the community (Para Social Work I Manual 2007, revised 2011).

III. Creation of First School of Social Work and Professional Associations in Tanzania

The Institute of Social Work is the first government institute in Tanzania, which offered social work education for quite a long time. The Institute of Social Work was established by Miscellaneous Act No. 3 of 2002 that amended the Act of Parliamentary No. 26 of 1973, which established the former National Social Welfare Training Institute. It provides training, consultancy services, and conduct research. The Institute of Social Work was accredited by the National Council for Technical Education (NACTE) to provide National Technical Awards

(NTA) from certificate, ordinary diploma, and degree programs in areas of social work and industrial relations and human resources management, and postgraduate diploma in social work and in law, mediation, and arbitration.

The Institute of Social Work started with the Department of Social Work in 1974. It is the founding and oldest academic department of the institute. The department was entrusted with the task of training social workers—most of whom were government employees employed under the Department of Social Welfare. In that regard, it was charged with the responsibilities of training qualified manpower that would have the capacity to strengthen the workforce that existed in Tanzanian society since the colonial rule.

The department started to offer ordinary diploma in social work in 1975. In 1977, the institute started to offer advanced diploma in social work, and in 1979, the certificate course started. In 1999, the Institute of Social Work also started to offer postgraduate diploma in social work managed by the internal structure of the institute as provided in the act that established the institute. The same act gave the institute the mandate to administer examinations and awards certificates as approved by the board of governors (Institute of Social Work 2011).

The Institute of Social Work is producing between 205–506 students per year in the field of social work. The increase of enrollment has been increasing since 2010 due to increase of awareness of the social work profession throughout the country. The Institute of Social Work has been advertising its programs through para social work training and the revitalization of the Tanzania Social Work Association (TASWA) in 2010. TASWA is closely associated with social workers who worked with the Department of Social Welfare. As such, TASWA had close relationship with the Ministry of Health and Social Welfare. TASWA has many activities, and most of the activities focus on two main objectives: first is to advocate social work practice as the profession, and second is to develop professional management practices, including budgeting and administration of the association for further development of the association. This has helped the association to enhance membership ownership of the organization and transparency of management.

In addition to programs offered at the Institute of Social Work, the Department of Social Welfare under the Ministry of Health and Social Welfare, in collaboration with the Institute of Social Work, are offering certificate program specifically designed for para social workers. The program is called Social Welfare Assistant Certificate Program where its graduates will be employed to the new cadre of welfare assistant at the ward levels.

IV. Development of TESWEP Project in Tanzania

Due to an increase demand of the social work professionals in Tanzania, the Institute of Social Work, in collaboration with Jane Addams College of Social Work, realized that some schools were offering social work education at various places in Tanzania. The partnership thought that it was important for universities and colleges to share information and harmonize and standardize their curricula so that those colleges and universities would be able to offer quality social work education that is in standard with international guidelines of social work profession. Therefore, Tanzania Emerging Schools of Social Work Program (TESWEP) was developed, and the goal was to review social work curricula in colleges and universities and enhancement of social work faculty development opportunities.

Currently, twelve schools are members of this program. A bachelor degree curricula have already been harmonized, and other four schools, including the Institute of Social Work, are developing masters in social work programs.

V. Strengthening the Social Welfare Workforce

Currently, the government of Tanzania is using the decentralization policy, which is used to recruit and place social welfare officers at the district level. This has been a responsibility of local authorities to recruit a new cadre of social welfare assistants at the ward level to supervise and support PSWs at the village level. Social welfare assistants will then be supervised and supported by district social welfare officers who are government employees.

District Council
Social Welfare District Level
Officers

Social Welfare Assistants
    Ward Level
PSW Field Supervisors

Most Vulnerable Children Committees
    Village Level
Community Volunteers
Paraprofessional Social Worker Trainees

Efforts to strengthen the social welfare force in Tanzania have faced a number of challenges. The challenges include shortage of social workers at the district, ward, and village levels. The few trained social workers mostly choose to work in private sectors, such as NGOs and other better paying industries and programs. This has affected the government sector to lack sufficient social workers who could be employed by central government. Another challenge is related to unknown profile of the social welfare department and its roles and functions and how social welfare services contribute to the overall development agenda in Tanzania. Social work profession has been continuously mixed up with other fields, such as development studies, community development, and sociology; hence creating more confusion to the social welfare delivery and resource distribution to the vulnerable groups in Tanzania. The social welfare services remains a low priority for governments' investment, hence the continuation of the underutilization of the social welfare services in Tanzania.

Chapter 3

Global Education

Introduction

Epistemology for Global Education

Developing an epistemology for educating globally ready social work students is nonfunctional without a sense of global realities of social development issues. Instructors combine activities, readings, workshops, and seminars as a way to assist in introducing a global mindset. The question is how will such educational practices facilitate a practitioners growth and understanding of cultural intervention skills needed when groups of culturally different people are mixing and migrating? What is the social work practice for ethnic violence, such as that in Kergestayn, or violence that crosses the borders between Mexico and US. One might call this behavior maladaptive cloistering where one culture is in the midst of another culture and faces discrimination, social development problems, and other concerns.

Study Abroad

What culturally specific social diagnostic tools are there for the practitioner to use that might assist? It is at this point that one wants the practitioner to be able to access culture knowledge acquired during a foreign study abroad or internship experience, thereby integrating the practitioner's understanding and treatment possibilities. Studying abroad allows social work students to study impediments to social development among various cultural groups, in comparison to social development in their native lands, thereby creating treatment models to help from within the client's culture.

Social Networking and Social Work

Use of social networking tools is a good beginning practice for enabling the communication process. For example, instant messaging can serve as a vehicle to collaborate across timelines in less than formal environments. If opportunity affords faculty members to before breakfast after dinner, these times may be a leisurely creative and productive environment for a coming together.

Emai summaries of these conversations serve as reminders, thought stimulators, outlines, and planning tools.

Video Teleconferencing/Videocam

The visual adds personality, structure, discipline, and professionalism. It holds promise for global education, exchange, and sharing among and across disciplines, universities, and continents—developing, expanding, and deepening global exchanges into the future.

In today's society, social networking and technology has reinforced the need for social work to be even increasingly involved with social networking culture and its global options for social work education.

Impact of Social Networking on Social Work Practice

Social scientists must monitor the impact of social media on priority areas of concern, such as mental health, learning, communication patterns, families, and education. Use of the social networking and technology resources among the young and the elderly has yet an undocumented story to tell about contributions as well as their contraindications for use with and for these groups.

We might begin by using social networking tools and skills to facilitate global education forums, and use the technologies to provide off-site supervision on culture, diagnosis, and treatment. No doubt, there are many unknowns to this new and evolving frontier.

Social work's pace has to quicken and research the impact of these communication changes, some expected but many unexpected, on the present day society. We are all cognizant of the work of the National Association of Social Workers, the International Association of Schools of Social Work, the International Federation of Social Workers, and others working globally to facilitate social justice on the world stage. Yet there has to be greater inclusion of those persons, theories, and methodologies from the periphery to the core. Social networking can be a contributor.

With inclusion in mind as we send our social work student around, we educate them and encourage them to critically examine opportunities to make meaningful cultural contributions to the profession, which will facilitate global social work practice.

Technology

I have come to the conclusion that I am totally infatuated with my iPad. This infatuation began because I liked the weight, size, and its portability. The idea that I could slide it into my pocket book was just too much for me. Now I spend my spare time, learning how to use the features. I am involved in a research project through the university that gave various faculty members an iPad. We will participate in discussion groups on now each of the participants has used their iPad.

Feature number one for me is to be able to write my email in the evening and have them sent when I tap into WiFi, thus giving me opportunity to compose thoughtful discussions and to revise if necessary

Expect the Unexpected

Expect the unexpected when arranging overseas travel for your students and yourself. Events and activities just don't work out the way they are written on paper. First of all, it never occurred to me that the department chair taking over from the one with whom I had arranged, the original agreement, had never implemented such a program previously. I assumed he had, and that put both of us at a disadvantage when it came to actually working out the particulars of day-to-day activities for the students involved. Therefore, the actual planning and implementation process only began just before my arrival. Fortunately, a PhD student who had participated in the program previously returned home for the summer and was assigned the job as coordinator of the project. Thankfully, I went a week early.

Another factor to consider is orientation of accompanying faculty members, who are unfamiliar with international travel, cultural aspects of the host county, the host faculty, and more. This situation puts one in several roles.

First, you are liaison to the host program. Second, you are the person who orientates both faculty member and students. It is entirely probable that you will end up providing two sets of orientation and not doing a great job at either. My situation turned into a duel schedule, whereby I actually had to take the accompanying faculty member to all points of interest prior to accompanying the students because the faculty person planned to stay only one week of the three-week program. Therefore, we went on tours, met with university administrators, and more. These dueling activities left the students feeling like I had abandoned them to this very new and culturally different environment.

Food for thought also is careful consideration of student capacity for thriving and learning in a foreign environment. How does one judge? The multitude of questions asked by the department of international education failed to predict the student who left for home after one week. The student responds to cold or insufficient water, tropical bugs, and the use of local transportation. It is extremely important to arrange a schedule for processing the student experience. Although several meetings were held prior to travel where handouts, discussions, and guest speakers participated, ongoing in country processing of the day to day experience is necessary. This helps to bring the fantasy of the trip into the real life experiences of each student.

If this sounds a bit overwhelming, it is, but take heart. It does get better with practice, insight, and analysis for change and refinement.

International Education Process

Personal travel, research, and cultural interests were a great starting point for student growth toward international social work education. I had been involved in several international study programs abroad during my PhD studies. Although they were no longer than three months at a time, that was just enough time to identify cultural interests, make informal relationships, and generate research ideas with a plan for funding them. Imagine the juxtapositioning of multiculturalism, cultural competence, as well as the emphasis on global readiness in education.

I revisited places where I had developed relationships and received added value to my international social work expertise. I called this expertise my social work tool bag. One of these places was the University of Dar es Salaam's Department of Fine and Performing Arts. There were summers of outreach in rural villages, script writing, theater development, and language studies. Theater was one means of studying social development. Theater techniques were used to educate and intervene with village problems. Poverty, rural isolation, lack of social services, gender issues, and lack of food security, water and power issues were included.

Although worthwhile, I couldn't quite decide on a US population with whom I would use it until I began paying closer attention to US emigrates coming from faraway places that understood the power of theater as a development tool. Such places are India, Africa, and South America.

Fayetteville State, now has a memorandum of understanding with UDSM Tanzania. The administrative approval process waded through two administrations, endless inquiries about why Tanzania, and questions about the proper wording to make sure we were not committing ourselves financially. So be prepared to be flexible and to defend.

At the same time, we had to make sure that those on the other end of this process understand that you value what they have to offer and that you are a contributor to their academic needs via research, publications, and exchanges. In other words, you are a worker bee, working hard to find funding resources and to make sure these resources are shared.

All of the above works better if everyone can put a face on the person with whom one collaborates. Remember, we went through two administrations; therefore, you must believe in the value of what you are trying to do. It may involve a few out-of-pocket trips on your part (you lucky dog) because others change administrators also, and you want them to know who you are, what your program involves, and its importance to their administration.

Hone your intelligence skills around campus. Sooner or later, someone will put a bug in your ear about needing to spend down their budget or some upcoming funding and the need for input from you. Of course, you have two proposal versions ever ready. Now, don't forget about the research and the publication. I know, I know, but you gotta do it. For example, I am writing this article on an iPad in Tanzania, which is somebody's research project All he does is monitor iPad usage.

So, what is the plan? Well, it might help if you have made your visits. You then know the program can better visualize what you want to do, and if others know you, you can get information, help, and ideas. Don't forget to write them into the proposal. Now, with funded proposal in hand, the real work begins.

Bajaji

Bajajis are these two-seated bikes of a sort. The first time I saw them used for transportation was when I went to a conference on San Andres Island, Colombia, and in movies. There are now hundreds of them around the town and waiting for you at the mall. I have used them several times between the mall and the bed and breakfast in which I stay. The drivers are males, serious about their work, and fast movers. These small businessmen in Tanzania are cautious drivers and good for short halls. This unusual site is new since I was last here. The mall is also new, with up-to-date shops, food courts, phones, and money exchange services. Road improvements, building starts, shopping malls, etc. are indicators of growth, even though the country is still very poor and 80 percent rural. The government is putting money into agriculture, education, and more. A plan to build a new medical school in Mlonganzila village is helping one of my village friends because they are compensating him for taking his land. Therefore, he has almost completed two small concrete homes. Each home has several rooms, one for each wife, to replace his mud and wood compound. But he also has two teenagers and grandchildren living with him. These new homes would have been impossible had he not received compensation.

Now, I have another friend who is a retired university agricultural worker. He lives in the village also and is fairly comfortable. He continues to work contracts for the university and other companies. Both men are over sixty and I believe may benefit differently from progress in their village. The latter's wife has a little shop, and his kids are grown, educated, and employed. One son also has a modern home in the village. He won't benefit from compensation but may benefit from growing his wife's shop. My adopted son also has a plan. He has several degrees, a fantastic job as the director of arts and culture, and two children with another on the way. He has built his home and started three rentals for medical school personnel or students. He is planning a bajaji business in the Kibamba area where he lives because there are no bajajis in that area.

I am trying to provide the students with opportunities to understand varying levels of social development during their visit.

Money Talks

Today the students and I left Tanzania. I find myself ready to get home and into my own bed. The stay was good because I saw a lot of friends and the students had many opportunities to learn about development issues in Tanzania and to make friends of their own. Always after one of these trips, I think about what I've learned. And frankly, I seem to be more convinced that the greater the differences the greater the similarities. I will give you one example. There were six of us traveling. We left campus at seven o'clock in order to make an 11:30 p.m. flight. The traffic is horrific. We got to the airport about 9:00 p.m. and immediately got into line. Then it dawned on me that each of us might be seen by a different KLM agent. So I asked one of the airport workers if he could assist me in getting us in as a group now. The idea of standing on that line for another hour or so is just too much for me.

The gentleman asked if he took care of me would I take care of him, I told him yes, not realizing that I did not have the TSh40 that I promised him. In any case, he spoke with the ticket agent, and we were told to get on her line. One of the students mentioned that I had the hookup again. It was a bit funny because I remembered coming back with some of these same students from New York in March. There, I'd gotten a Red Cap to check our bags and put us on the train early so the students could have their choice of seat. The wheeling and dealing, I think I inherited that from my father. He was a master, and I watched him carefully for daddy's tips worked, and they do for me as well.

To make a long story short, the students put in about $23.00 in US currency plus the T shillings I had. We were not charged for our extra 300 lb. in weight. They chose their seats, moved ahead in line, and even had time to relax and shop a bit more before the real crowds gathered. New York or Dar es Salaam money talks.

Issues Related to Women

One focus of international social work education is the lives of women in the developing world. International organizations, such as the World Health Organization (WHO) and the Center for Disease Control (CDC), have begun to examine abuse of women in Africa. Organizational studies have informed social scientists worldwide about cultural, religious, and social factors that impact the abuse phenomena.

The study of individual countries facilitates social work education for students who are unable to participate in international internships and travel experiences. Because of its unique demographics, traditional ethnic groups, religions, and urban and rural cultures, Tanzania, with approximately thirty-three million, people is a diverse nation. Yet it is still one of the poorest nations in the world. Tanzania is democratic and lives in peace with its neighboring countries in East Africa.

When studying abuse in Tanzania and look at how the CDC describes abuse reflects the current thinking. Abuse or what is frequently termed as intimate partner violence (IPV) can be physical, sexual, or psychological by a current or former partner or spouse.

Physical violence is an attempt to cause harm, disability, or death. Sexual violence is a sexual act against the will of another person. Psychological abuse is victim humiliation, controlling what the victim can and cannot do, withholding information from the victim, deliberately doing something to make the victim feel diminished or embarrassed, isolating the victim from friends and family, and denying the victim access to money or other basic resources.

The University of Dar es Salaam's Department of Fine and Performing Arts uses participatory theater when researching the lives of women in Tanzania. This research model enables facilitators to access intimate knowledge of social factors as they impact the lives of residents. Participatory theater utilizes the subject being studied in the research process.

As a student of participatory theater research in Tanzania, the subject of relationships between men and women living in Tanzania was intriguing. Women spoke of themselves as less than partners in marriage, frequently explaining how their hopes and dreams for bettering their lives had been suppressed in service to their husbands without creative, intellectual, or other social options. When asked if other women in the village identified similar feelings, the answer was often yes; however, few spoke of it openly. Men controlled their wives ability to speak and interact with others freely, their ability to travel, and their ability to seek upward mobility. In group conversations, men and women interacted separately. The men were secure in their position as leaders of the village and their families. It was easy as a facilitator to fall into the pattern of men speaking with the men, and women with the women only. Special efforts had to be made to share the information and plan interventions that were appropriate.

The conversations shared by the women were topics, such as rape, circumcision rituals, fear of HIV/AIDS, and the sexual rights of men outside of marriage. The range of these conversations could not be shared with their husbands based on their nature. Wives were limited because of cultural norms and religious practices. Men were controlling, and most were Muslim, both severely limited the types and quality of communication between males and females. Very creative ways were used to insure that wives were not alienated. Wives tactfully made sure that the researchers knew secrets of their husband's personality. We could therefore plan an approach.

A specific issue raised was that in one village, only thirty-five miles north of Dar es Salaam was not far from an established army base. This proved to be problematic for men and women in different ways. The men were worried because the base threatened to take over their lands for expansions. The women were concerned about this, but theirs were other concerns that had not been shared with the men. The soldiers were raping the women when they went to do their gardening. They felt that they could not tell their husbands without being accused of facilitating these opportunities for rape. The dangers involved in changing the order and sharing this information through the research and theater intervention projects being facilitated were enormous.

As in the literature, there were many stories of power, sexual exploitation, and abuse. The literature suggests that education, fertility, and dowry play significant roles in frequent incidences of abuse.

Interest in the plight of African women suffering abuse has been a subject for investigation from several angles. Randall (2003) writes about domestic violence in the African context, and identifies at least six African countries where studies of the condition have taken place since the 1990s. Randall (2003) also identifies theories of domestic violence that appear in African literature. The World Health Organization (2000–2003) has conducted its own study of women in eleven countries. Tanzania was among those linking bride-price to abuse.

The aim of the research is to extend knowlege of female abuse in Tanzania by examining contributing social factors. The research questions will examine eight social factors: age, education, income, location, mobility, polygamy, religion, and sterility.

In spite of household population surveys in Latin America, Southeast Asia, and Africa, few, if any, surveys have established the population rate based of intimate partner violence in Tanzania. Needed is a more profound understanding of gender violence in Tanzania and the factors that contribute to that violence. Frequent use of the terms gender violence, intimate partner violence, and abuse are used interchangeably in describing environments hostile to the health, mental health, and welfare of women in Tanzania. Although data on abuse are sparse, rates of prevalence have been assessed in many undeveloped areas of the world. Some African countries, where data are available, include rural Uganda, Zimbabwe, South Africa, Zambia, and Sierra Leone. Partner violence is seen by 53 percent of the women in Sub-Saharan Africa as an acceptable condition of their lives.

Tanzania's population is approximatly 62 million with a cultural blend of African, Arab, European, and Indian influences. The African people of Tanzanians represent approximately 120 tribal groups. The population the largest group is of Bantu origin. With twenty-six administrative divisions, Tanzania is one of the least urbanized countries in Sub-Saharan Africa." Tanzania's border countries are Burundi, Democratic Republic of the Congo, Kenya, Malawi, Mozambique, Rwanda, Uganda, and Zambia. The religions are Christian, 30 percent; Muslim, 35 percent; indigenous beliefs, 35 percent; and Zanzibar, more than 99 percent. Muslim literacy rate is average, 78.2 percent, with ages fifteen and over able to read and write Kiswahili (Swahili), English, or Arabic.

Theoretical Framework

The theoretical framework is drawn from one of five theories that occur in African literature on domestic violence. These theories are the rights theories, feminist theories, cultural explanations, society-in-transition explanations, and culture of violence explanations. Cultural explanation theory explains the domestic violence incidents within Tanzanian culture. The cultural explanation points to the uneven power issues of traditional marriage, polygamy, male promiscuity as an acceptable circumstance, the extended family power connection, and the wide spread use of dowry or bride-price.

Cultural theories of domestic violence embrace husband dominance, traditional roles for women, and violence as a means of enforcing these traditional roles. Violence fosters the treatment of women as property, socializes passivity, and polygamy lessons of a wife's bargaining power.

Hypothesis

The study attempted to identify and explain women's vulnerability to abuse by her husband or significant other. What factors contribute to the prospects for abuse of women in Tanzania is the focus. Variables examined are urban or rural residence, age, length of marriage/relationship, education, religion, number of children, ability to conceive, and ability to make financial contributions to the relationship.

Abuse Issue

The issue of violence has implications for international social work practice and education. The subject has had some degree of study in Tanzania, which sites abuse as directly influencing women's health, empowerment, social justice, and other social work practice areas. The Tanzanian Technical Report (2004–2005) sites the following as it relates to abuse of women in Tanzania:

Some men and women report that there are times when violence is justified. Some of those times are

- when your female partner is unfaithful;
- when your female partners will not tell the truth about something; and
- when a female partner has refused sex for a long time, her partner feels it is right for him to use force to have sex with her.

During the years of 2000–2003, twenty-four thousand women in eleven residents of Global South countries were surveyed to assess their experiences of violence. The special focus of this questionnaire was on intimate partner violence. The definition used for partner violence was "the woman had been slapped or had something thrown at her; pushed or shoved; hit with a fist or something else that could hurt; kicked, dragged or beaten up; choked or burnt; threatened with or had a weapon used against her." Tanzania participated in the study utilizing collaborating institutions Muhimbili University College of Health Sciences and the Women's Research and Documentation Project of the University of Dar es Salaam. The instrument used was developed and validated for cross-cultural use. Individual interviews of women ages fifteen to forty-nine (N-1820) in Dar es Salaam and (N-1450) in Mbeya district were conducted.

Findings show 33 percent of women with partners in Dar es Salaam had experienced physical violence compared to 47 percent in Mbeya. Severe abuse experiences were 17 percent in Dar es Salaam compared to 25 percent. Severe abuse for this study was defined as "being hit with a fist or something else, kicked, dragged, beaten up, choked burnt on purpose, threatened with a weapon, or had a weapon used against them." The study found that 29 percent of the women who experienced violence were injured. Fifteen percent in Dar es Salaam and 23 percent in Mbeya lost consciousness at least once as a result.

Abuse of women is considered a public health problem by many researchers. It is not only necessary to assess the impact of abuse on the woman but, if pregnant, on the health of the child as well. Physical violence during pregnancy was addressed in the survey of Tanzanian women. Pregnant women in Dar es Salaam were beaten during pregnancy. Seven percent were beaten during at least one pregnancy. Of that group, 38 percent reported being kicked or punched in the abdomen. In Mbeya, the percentages were twelve and twenty-three respectively. Beating of this group was more severe during pregnancy.

In Dar es Salaam, women who had experienced abuse reported more health problems than those women who did not experience abuse. The likelihood of having thoughts of suicide was reported at twice the rate of women who had not experienced abuse.

There are additional considerations to any consideration of abuse of Tanzanian women. According to IRIN, in a 2006 project of the UN, women reported non-partner violence by women beginning at ages as young as fifteen years. Teachers as perpetrators were identified by over half of all women who reported abuse in this category.

Still a more subtle component of the culture that contributes to abuse is the paying of a bride-price/dowry. The practice is identified as a contributing factor facilitating abusive behavior. Research in Tanzania has shown that the perception is that the abuser has paid for and owns the woman. While researchers did not go deep into the villages, however, out of 725 interviews, 439 of the women were interviewed from the capital of Dar es Salaam and nine other regions in Tanzania. While the findings are applicable in the more urban areas, it begs the question, what are the factors that influence abuse in the lives of village women in Tanzania?

Schellenberg, et al. (2003) conducted a study on the health of children in rural southern Tanzania in which they described the living environment of a rural region that covered the Kilombero, Morogoro Rural, Rufiji, and Ulanga districts of southern Tanzania.

This region has a population of one to two million people in a fertile flood plain with most people existing as subsistence farmers. Major crops include rice, maize, cassava, millet, sesame, coconut, and cashews nuts. Houses have corrugated or thatched roofs with wood-framed mud walls. Although income was difficult to determine because large numbers were involved in farming, 26 percent of Tanzanian families lived on one dollar per day from 1990 to 1996. "In Kilombero and Ulanga, the median value of monthly household consumption and expenditure in 1997 in a sample of local households was under $100-of which about 75% was for food."

The description of the rural areas of Tanzania gives the researcher a limited understanding of the difficulties of rural living. Many residents of the Global South live in similar village environments. Many of these women are subject to several forms of violence, with domestic violence being the most notorious. Studies were conducted by UC Davis Biologist Tim Caro and Anthropologist Monique Borgerhoff Mulder to answer such questions as "Why do women and men stay in marriages or divorce and how these decisions do affect their families?" Their findings demonstrated that economics play a vital role in shaping men's and women's marital and reproductive strategies. McCloskey, et al. (2005) identified several factors that may contribute to partner violence in Tanzania. These factors were "incomplete education (under 8th grade), having many children, and child sexual abuse."

Contributing Factors for Abuse among Rural Women

Factor one of the Bangladesh study showed that education of the wife was an important factor. With increased education of the wife, there was less risk for abuse. However, there were also some studies cited that showed partner violence was related to higher levels of the husband's education and others that seemed to imply that the level of higher education for both partners was significant in determining education.

A few studies found a significantly reduced risk of physical abuse by the husband partner with increasing education of the wife and with very low rates where the wife is highly educated. Some studies show lower violence levels when one or both spouses have been educated at least through secondary school. Other studies show that the risk of domestic violence is related to higher levels of husband's education (Profamilia 1995; Evaluation Project 1997; Schuler, et al. 1996; Jeieebhov and Cook 1997; and Visaria 1998).

Women's Autonomy/Status

While mobility was associated positively with violence, marrying later in life was shown to significantly lower the risk of violence along with having greater control over family resources.

One study showed the higher age at marriage by the wife and greater control over resources was associated with significantly lower risks of domestic violence. Increased mobility by women was positively associated with violence (Jeieebhov and Cook 1997).

Socioeconomic Status and Dowry/Bride-Price

Higher socioeconomic status and/or caste, as well as a large dowry, having an inverse relationship to partner abuse with the dowry/bride factor showing significance, have been generally found to be inversely related to risk of domestic violence (Profamilia 1995; Evaluation Project 1997; Schuler, et al. 1996; Jeieebhov and Cook 1997; and Visaria, 1998).

Dowry/Bride-Price

The large dowry given to the husband is significantly inversely related to the risk of domestic violence in India (Jeieebhov and Cook 1997).

Familial and Parental Support

Studies in South India and Cambodia demonstrate that the presence of the wife's brothers were inversely related to reported domestic violence. In Cambodia, domestic violence was 20 percent lower if the couple resided with the wife's parents (Nelson and Zimmerman, 1996).

Income/Economic Group Membership

Bangladesh studies showed that membership in group-based savings and credit programs was associated with significantly lower rates of domestic violence. However. the group factor was not as significant as the wife's enhanced status within the family, though she demonstrated ability to bring home a sought–after resource. such as credit loans (Schuler, et al. 1996).

Situational Factors

Factors such as alcohol and wife sterilization (fidelity) were significant factors for increased domestic violence (Rao 1977; Hoffman, et al. 1994; Nelson and Zimmerman 1996; and Profamilia 1995).

Contextual and Community Factors

There is some evidence indicating considerable heterogeneity across communities with respect to levels of domestic violence. In a Baltimore, United States, study, the authors found several contextual variables measuring neighborhood poverty, unemployment, and home ownership were all significantly related to women's risk of domestic violence, after controlling for individual and familial factors (Schuler, et al. 1996; Evaluation Project 1997; and O'Campo, et al. 1995).

Conclusion

Ghana, Tanzania, and South Africa were the first African countries to begin an in-depth look at the problem of domestic violence. In the mid-'90s, these countries began anecdotal, informal, and formal surveys on such topics as partner abuse and femicide. Similarly, in Ghana, Uganda, and Kenya, activists began lobbying for legal protection or codes, which only South Africa and Mauritius have passed. Organizations were set up to counsel women in Zimbabwe and South Africa. Non-governmental organizations (NGOs) have established shelters for abused women in Mauritius, Nigeria, and Senegal, while Ghana and South Africa now have domestic abuse units within the police force for women and children.